Tales of All the Forest
And All of the Meadow

By
S. Oliver Scrapp

A Framework Document for
A   E   O
I and U

Dedicated to Mr Pixie Plip

Chapter 1

In the morning when the sun comes up, and all the birds and the animals wake up, funny things happen in the forest and the meadow. When the grass wakes up, it sleepily squeezes tiny droplets out to make a frosting breakfast drink for Pixie Pod. Pixie Pod usually wakes up a little bit later than the other animals.

This is because Pixie Pod's mushroom house is

underneath the biggest oldest oak tree in the forest. And so when the sun comes up, it doesn't reach Pod's windows straight away. This particular morning Pixie Pod woke up on the wrong side of the bed, and falling to a heap on the floor, he didn't know which way to turn. Normally Pixie Pod would have had his breakfast first, but today being what it was, the silly pixie went and made his dinner first. He put carrots and potatoes in the pot and put his eating things on the table. Tree Topper Clive was at this time at the other side of the forest starting a normal day by eating some nuts, having got out of the bed on the right side. Tree Topper Clive didn't have a home as such, especially as one nut tree is as good as the next, which is better than none in squirrel-land. And occasionally when it became too cold for Clive to climb the trees, there was always the store of nuts Pod would leave under the mat, just in case, but not usually in the morning time.

After dinner, Pixie Pod sat down by the stove and read his favourite bedtime story to himself. "Terrible Timmy and the Mad Bad Bumps". He scratched his head. 'Hmmm' he said to himself, 'normally when I have my bedtime read, I get so tired by the middle of the story that I never make it to the end, How Strange!!'. Pixie Pod then thought that a wander through the woods would set him straight. So with further adon't , Pod was hat,coat and gloves out the door.

Pod didn't notice the bright sunlight bouncing off the dew drops when he made it to the meadow, so as far as he was concerned, it was still evening. Although by this time, the whole of the forest and the meadow was busy being the whole of the forest and the meadow, and very much alive and awake.

Pixie Pod was bored with the walk. Something wasn't right about the day and doing what he was doing, wasn't solving the problem, so he turned and plodded home. On the way he began thinking about what he should do. He should do something as it was Trinkday, the thrumteenth day of the week and Pixie Pod had never known a Trinkday before when there was nothing to be done. Pixie Pod reached his front door and went back inside.

'Right!' he said, 'Lunch!!' to himself. Today being today consisted of Gloobleberry muffins and tea. Normally lunch wouldn't be Gloobleberry muffins and tea, it's just that Pixie Pod was so confused, that when he tried to think of food, all he could think of was Gloobleberries. Anyway, he made lunch.

As Pixie Pod was sitting down to lunch, there was a knock at the door. Twas Tree Topper Clive dropping in to say hello. "Would you join me and have some Gloobleberry muffin?", asked Pod. "How kind of you to offer", said Tree Topper Clive, as he sat up to the table. Tree Topper Clive was having a normal day and eating anything other than nuts was strange for him. So Clive didn't assume to think that Pod was having anything other than a normal day himself.

They ate muffin and chatted, and when lunch was over, he said "Thank you very much" to Pod and bid him farewell, as he had important business with important squirrels to attend to. Pod was the only pixie in the whole of the forest and the meadow, so there were no important pixie meetings ever. Pixie Pod was now more confused than ever, and the mushroom house was a big mess. "Time to clean up, I suppose", he grumbled to himself. Attending to the kitchen, he went straight to the sink, throwing everything that was dirty into a mountain of dirty things in the sink. "Hot water and suds", sang Pod as the mountain of dirty things made their way to the draining board, and not by magic either!!

By the time Pixie Pod was finished in the clean kitchen, the sun was setting out the kitchen window. Pixie

Pod was now more confused than ever about something, so he sat down for a moment to think about what to do, and do you know what he did next? No! Well he fell fast asleep in his stove side seat. When he woke up it was dark and the stove had gone out.

Later on he woke up again and yawned. "What was it about today that made it so different from most of my other days?", he said to himself, but of course he was on his own, so he didn't expect an answer. He went to the nut jar to leave some nuts out for Tree Topper Clive, but strangely he discovered Tree Topper Clive's nuts from the previous night already under the mat. So he put the nuts back into the nut jar, drank a glass of milk and got back into the wrong side of the bed and fell fast asleep.

Chapter 2

Tree Topper Clive happened to be dandering along the outskirts of the meadow, one day, which also happened to be the outskirts of the forest depending on which way you heard it. Pixie Pod tended to hear it every which way, but that was neither here nor there. Tree Topper Clive was examining all the nut trees, pondering which one to climb next, as they all seemed to have spiky green round things on their branches. Tree Topper Clive did not fancy the idea of being launched to the ground by a low velocity conker shell.

The dangers of being a squirrel are not entirely apparent to the casual pixie, but upon inspection, bigger animals with hungrier tummies and even bigger winds with their warms and chills are all prone to perilous situations for the wayward squirrel. Tree Topper Clive thought to himself, 'What I should really like now, more than everything else in the whole forest, is a nice dry branch in the sun's path, some nuts that carry no price, and perhaps only for the night, another squirrel to want for my company'. "Sigh", said Tree Topper Clive, "I know if I wasn't me, I'd like me for a friend".

Suddenly, there it was, a tree without any spiky green things growing from it. So he climbed with haste, to deep within the tree, where he found an empty nest. The leaves and the branches formed a clearing upwards from the nest to reveal the sky. Tree Topper Clive climbed into the nest and he could feel a warmth, just as if there were someone there a few moments previous. The nest was shaped just as if it was meant to be an armchair built for someone with a body like Tree Topper Clive's. just so such a body could sit in warmth and comfort while at the same time look through the tunnel in the tree to the sky.

"Hello", said a voice as Clive firmly rooted himself in the nest. Clive would have jumped but for the fact, he was more reclined in comfort now than he ever imagined possible, if that's possible?

"Eh Hi", said the squirrel not knowing who, why, what or how he was saying "Hi" to. There wasn't exactly anything to say "Hi" to as far as the eye could see. So Clive chose not to continue looking but instead to say, "How do you be doing?"

- Oh I don't be doing, was the reply, I do be being

- Oh that's terribly nice, said Clive, anxious to be jovial about the situation

- What is terribly nice?

- Well it is when something is so nice, it is terribly nice, Clive stated

- Is nice the same as being?

- hmmm, I suppose it all depends on where you happen to be standing, or sitting for that matter, thought Clive. Clive then had a startling thought. Who am I talking to?

- Me, said the tree

- Huh? Said Tree Topper Clive

-        Oh yes, very much so and indeed thereupon, why don't you stay for a while, I'm feeling quite lonely as a tree, and the nest that you are sitting in has been abandoned for some time.

-        Do you know, I think I shall, thank you very much, said Clive with a smile.

With that Clive began to doze, but not quite fall asleep. It was as if a dream was beginning. A dream that if you asked him afterwards, he wouldn't be quite able to put into words. Tree Topper Clive wasn't very good when it came to words, anyhows, nuts were his speciality. If there ever came to be a school for all the forest and the meadow, Tree Topper Clive would surely be the nut teacher. Therein, all the squirrel children could come to school and become wise in the way of nuts. Was this his dream?

The tree gestured a thought, 'Perhaps I may be so bold as to offer my assistance in your quest for nuts?' "How?" asked Tree Topper Clive. 'Well if its nuts that you need, I have some right here'. Just at that moment, Clive's eyes fell on some nuts hanging from a nut branch just behind him. "Why, thank you", said Clive as he picked the biggest and juiciest nut. 'Are you going to eat the nut just like that?', inquired the tree. "I suppose I am", said Clive. He bit a large bite from the nut and thought to say, "Do you happen to know any other trees that talk?" "Ah that would be telling", said the tree "anyway", continued the tree, "I don't know very many trees to talk to, and I wouldn't know what other trees looked like at the other side of the forest". "Aha I see", said Clive. "Do you?", murmured the tree.

Clive looked up through the clearing, night was beginning to fall or the sun was going down, whichever way you happened to be looking. All Clive could see though, was that the colour of the little bit of sky which he could see, was bright blue, was now quite grey, and

he assumed would shortly become very black. Maybe there would be a star or two to look at as well. "Fancy a bit of stargazing?" asked the tree to the now quiet weary squirrel. "What do you mean, look at two white blips hanging in the sky!" said Clive. "Oh yes, but only at night time, as it is now" said the tree.

Tree Topper Clive looked up into the sky, and his gaze fell upon the two stars he saw there shining brightly. He looked away then, but all was dark and he felt blind, so he looked up again. He was transfixed by the two white blips. "Do you stargaze?" inquired Tree Topper Clive of the tree. The tree said not as such, no. "You see I don't have eyes. I can't see but I can feel the stars being there in much the same way I feel you there in that abandoned nest. Would you like to know the story of the abandoned nest?" asked the tree. "Yes please" said Clive.

Chapter 3

"A few seasons ago, shall we say, a legendary magpie lived in the forest and the meadow. Napaleen I believe her name was, and she was an unloved bird. Napaleen felt that because she was an unloved bird, that indeed she wasn't worth loving. The more she thought this way, the more upset she became. Being upset, upset Napaleen, so she took to collecting things she stumbled across which she thought nice. These things all seemed to be shiny as it happened, so that when Napaleen put all her shiny pieces in the one place, a glow of light unimaginable became imaginables.

One day as Napaleen soared through the air she saw a shiny white blip in the meadow and she flew to it. She landed in the grass beside the shiny piece, which was also beside a hole in the ground. She took the piece and no notice of the hole, and made her way back to her nest here.

As she flew away, a white rabbit came out of the hole wondering where his mirror had gone. Damn those children, he muttered under his breath. Anyhow Napaleen came back here and put the mirror at the top of the shiny pile, and she stood back and looked at the pile. For the first time, she saw herself. Or more correctly, what she looked like to the naked eye. "Oh" she said to herself, "I'm all black with white bits, or is it all white with black bits.

This scared her and she flapped her wings violently, knocking all the shiny pieces out of the nest to the ground. She flew upwards beating her wings with all her might against all my branches and leaves in the way. And she did break through, leaving the hole to the sky you now see before you. That was the last of Napaleen I have since heard. I do hope she is happy now. So what do you think of that?" asked the tree.

Tree Topper Clive was fast asleep.

Chapter 4

Pixie Pod was sitting pretty pretty in the shade of the glum tree one fine Troopday, whereupon he pondered the misgivings Tree Topper Clive had been giving him.

Tree Topper Clive had been off weather of late you see, and Pixie Pod thought that it was himself being the source of all said unmirth. Unmirth cast grey clouds over all the forest and all the meadow. Grey clouds which seemed to just about hold back the mightiest and fiercest storms that ever fell upon this world we have come to know. Pod took no notice to these clouds as his notice was decidedly Tree Topper Clive's long faces.

Tree Topper Clive had been feeling grey himself for sometime, and the more he felt grey, the greyer he felt. Pod didn't like it when his friend carried this greyness and unmirth with him into all that he met and conversed with. Others that dwelled roundabout had cause to mention this to Pixie Pod, regarding him as Clive's closest friend. So that is how we came to be here in the shade of the glum tree, or more correctly reading Pixie Pod in the shade of the glum tree.

Tree Topper Clive returned from a particularly grey walk, during which it nearly rained thrice. So he gave a name to the path he walked such that all who walked that path afterwards would know its name. It was grey path. He came to the glum tree where Pod sat reflecting. "Hi Clive". "Hi Pod". Clive sat beside Pod.

"How are you my friend?" questioned the perplexed pixie. "Not too good Pod" said Clive. "I feel like the misery witch is following me everywhere I go, and the more I tell the misery witch to shoo, the colder I feel". "Well put a jumper on you silly squirrel" said Pixie Pod. "Will that make the misery witch go away?" said the quizzical squirrel. "Oh yes" said Pod quite matter-of-factly, "it is widely known", continued Pod "that misery witches in hot pursuit of cold squirrels, lose all their evil powers when the squirrels put a jumper on".

"But I don't have a jumper" said Clive. "Would you like to borrow one of mine?" said Pod. "Oh yes please" said Clive, trying to imagine what it would be like to not have any misery witches hot on his trail.

So up the two got and plodded back to the mushroom house, which wasn't in the shade of the glum tree. The two had to walk the other way from grey path to get to Pod's house, and when they got there, Pod saw that Clive's spirits were still down. Once inside the mushroom door, Pixie Pod grabbed Tree Topper Clive's attentions and demanded to know exactly how long it had been since the misery witch wouldn't leave him alone. "Ever since I spent that night in the talking tree" droned the shivering squirrel.

"Aha !" exclaimed Pixie Pod "where on fact in all the forest and the meadow did you happen to meet a talking tree. "Well not in the meadow you daft pixie" snapped Tree Topper Clive, angry at Pod for shedding dark on his wayward happening. "You see" he continued "when I stayed by the talking tree, I saw that it was really quiet very clever. So after hearing just how clever the talking tree was, I thought that I should introduce it, or her, or him, to my best friend, you. But when I went to get you, I got lost, so I tried to find the talking tree instead and I got more lost, and then I felt the misery witches running after me, and then I found you by the glum tree, and I'm still cold, and I still don't know where the talking tree is, and, and, and, BOOHOOHOO ......

Pixie Pod couldn't think what to say, but he felt very sorry for trying to tell Tree Topper Clive that trees didn't talk. In an effort to make peace with the sobbing squirrel Pixie Pod, went and fetched his warmest cuddliest woolly jumper. He came back from the upstairs of the mushroom house to put the woolly jumper over the by now very chilled Clive, and as luck would have it, some fresh Gloobleberry muffin happened to be handy on the stove.

The stove was cold, but it didn't take Pixie Pod very long to get a fire going, to make the mushroom house very cosy indeed. Whereupon he sat down by the muffined and warmed Tree Topper Clive and said "Please, if you would, tell me about the talking tree, because it seems you lost your way sometime after meeting this talking tree". Clive told Pod as much as he knew about the tree and about Napaleen magpie, which wasn't as much as we know. Still it was enough for Pixie Pod to understand why Tree Topper Clive became so glum when he couldn't find his way back to such a wonderful tree. He also remembered meeting a magpie called Napaleen once, which cheered Clive up somewhat.

After an evening of banter and warmth, Tree Topper Clive's spirits had perked up an awful lot, to the point in fact where he probably wouldn't even be able to remember glum path if he tried, as he didn't write it down at the time. Sleepiness crept into the mushroom house making the two friends drift off into snoresland with little contented grins on their faces, which probably meant they were having little contented dreams behind their tiny shut eyes. If you had been there, you might have said the Ayes have it, but you weren't, so when the morning came back around there wasn't one grey cloud to be seen in the blue sky above the whole of the forest and the meadow.

Chapter 5

While winter still had such cold weather, Tree Topper Clive didn't know whether he had goosebumps or boosegumps. Clive did realise however that he did not like the winter time, and maybe as a squirrel he wasn't meant to. For now it was o.k. to stay in Pixie Pod's mushroom house but he didn't want to put Pixie Pod out every time the wintertime came along.

Maybe if when the wintertime came by, I grew more skinfluff, like as if it were a jumper, or perhaps t'were a way of not being a squirrel, even in the wintertime, thought Clive. These were all very silly thoughts really, when the obvious solution would be to stop roaming the trees and settle down. "I could live in a mushroom house, but . . .", he said to himself, "it could only make me think I was a pixie, and I couldn't live in a nest for I'm not a bird and I don't want to think that neither". Tree Topper Clive had the whole of the rest of the winter to think up a suitable sort of a warm spot for the next winter so he wouldn't get the cold boosegumps, or was that it? The more Tree Topper Clive dreamt of a place to call home, the more he wished for a home to become his place.

Tree Topper Clive tried on a few occasions to go back and find the talking tree, but by now, none of the trees had any green spiky things growing from them. So it was quite impossible to tell which tree it was which talked instead of growing the green spiky things. Today, however, the ever watching squirrel was off in search of a home instead of a tree, and not specifically a home which talked. Clive looked like a squirrel full of hot air, as he left the mushroom house with Pixie Pod's big woolly jumper on. He bounced from tree to tree, each bounce meaning the last place wasn't suitable enough to live as a squirrel.

Many trees and many more bounces later, Clive came across a great big oak tree, with a deep hole in the middle of its bow. This cast ideas into Topper Clive's head about dream homes and such like. The hole itself looked like it was big enough to fit seven or eight Tree Topper Clives, and then some, which probably could be a space for nuts and muffin and whatever else he might eat as a progressive squirrel with a new home. The hole was buried deep into the heart of the soft of the tree, like a bubble of darkness that still kept the warmth of a living tree's insides. Tree Topper Clive went back outside to the ground and gathered some dead leaves that had gone all brown, and cracked all around the edges with a different sort of deader brown, and the edges were turned up a little bit too. So he took them back and made curtains for his new house, and a very intricate leaf cupboard for his nuts and tea service, and, of course, Gloobleberry muffin.

Tree Topper Clive sat in the hole in the tree, which by the way, had no leaves, for a very long time. . . and after another very long time, he came up with the idea of a Grimpalong for a name for his new home. The trouble was, he didn't know where he got the name Grimpalong as he had never heard anyone say Grimpalong before, but it sounded right. The amazing thing was, the more he thought it was a Grimpalong, the more comfortable and grimpy it felt.

It took exactly two bits of night time and two bits of dark time for Clive to turn his newly discovered hole in a tree into a perfectly functional Grimpalong. As soon as this was done, he ran straight to his best friend's mushroom house to invite Pixie Pod to high nuts and muffin. It should be pointed out that the muffin originally came from Pod's house as Clive himself couldn't foresee a clever way to put a cooker in a tree. Clive knocked on Pod's door.

"Fancy popping over to my new Grimpalong?" inquired Tree Topper Clive enthusiastically, "for some nuts and muffin, and tea, of course, if you have a tea bag, that is!". With that, the two set off to the new Grimpalong, bantering very happily as they went about this and that and of course, the other.

Sitting on a branch outside the front door of the Gloopalong, which also was part of the roof of the Gloopalong, the two sat. Pixie Pod with a mouthful of muffin on the nut sandwich said, "I wasn't exactly sure what you said a Gloopalong was, but I now think I understand what you meant", and took a bite from the sandwich. Tree Topper Clive, who at the time was a very self satisfied little squirrel, decided not to take a bite of his sandwich and instead looked up into the sky with a smile that was a squirrel's face wide. Pod went on to say, "Gloopalong is a very good name indeed for a home".

However with a bounce of notion, Tree Topper Clive turned to Pixie Pod and said quite matter-of-factly that what he was referring to was a Grimpalong and not indeed a Gloopalong. Gloopalong's were something completely different altogether. In another fact, in some parts of the meadow, not too far from white rabbit's home, Gloopalong is considered a bit of a rude word. Tree Topper Clive began thinking of rude words as he took a bite of nut sandwich.

The two stayed quite a long time after that, but not very long on the subject of rude words, as everyit is quite polite in the whole of the forest and the meadow. When the sun said "Good evening", Pixie Pod said his good evenings and his thank yous, and made his way back to the mushroom house. Clive sat for a little while more on the branch, ever so very happy about life, before retiring to the Grimpalong. Before he fell asleep, he had a very amusing thought. "Imagine if my very own Grimpalong happened to be the talking tree?"

Chapter 6

White Rabbit was terribly plagued by his children who always asked him to bring them on holidays and somesuch when they were bored. So one day he caved in and off the six rabbits marched with white rabbit driving the steering ears. Only white rabbits have steering ears by the way. White rabbit decided that because he didn't know very many places, that he should just lead them through the forest, which looked bigger than the meadow.

When they all got to the edge of the forest, there

were two ways for them to go. One of the ways was Glum path,

which white rabbit knew, because he was there that day, but because rabbits can't write, he couldn't be definite. So without mentioning Glum path, white rabbit chaired a vote on which path to take. Three quite partial rabbits chose this path against the two votes for that path, so they set off on this path which white rabbit had a nasty feeling about.

White rabbit's ears turned and headed off one by another down this path which had little bits of sun bursting through the branches that lived over this path. A few sunbursts later, white rabbit spied a river in the midst, so thought to not really say anything and take his steering ears to the back of the pack by saying "Oh look at that big tree!", and stopping to look at a big tree that happened to be there at the time. None of the other rabbits were bothered enough to stop to look at the tree, so it wasn't long later when white rabbit's steering ears happened to hear, "Oh look, what's that?"

White rabbit sighed, "Pixie Pod told me once that that was in fact a river".

"What's a Pixie Pod?", beamed the littlest rabbit. White rabbit giggled to himself, "Pixie Pod is another story all together, but what is important is that, that river thing is moving drink which sometimes falls out of the sky, and cannot be walked upon by rabbits, because they will just go down and stop being rabbits".

"How do we get over there so?", furthered the little rabbit.

White rabbit's face changed, "Eh, do we need to be on the other side of the river?"

"Well we have come this far and it would be a shame to turn back all because rabbits can't walk on rivers", grinned littlest rabbit.

White rabbit pondered, "maybe if we went someway along the river we might find something bigger than the river, that lives over the river, so what do you think we should do?"

"I think we should have another vote", said the littlest rabbit, "or maybe even two".

"What do you mean?", asked the white rabbit. The littlest rabbit then stated with all the other rabbits' attention, "What I think I mean is that we could vote on whether to go on or go back, and if it was decided that we should go on, do we then go this way or that, along the river".

Then white rabbit got up on his bum legs to get everyone else's attentions and said "Do you think that because I have leaded you this far, that now I don't have to lead you anymore, because you have come this far?"

The littlest rabbit didn't say anything but the other rabbits piped up a unanimous yes as they were all wondering which way to go up the river. So a vote was taken where it was decided that turning back was not to be, and in the second vote, two rabbits voted for a left turn, two rabbits voting for a right turn and white rabbit and littles rabbit not voting. White rabbit chose not to vote on the grounds that he was previously out voted in a matter he cared passionately for, he wanted to go home. The littlest rabbit didn't commit himself to a vote because he was copying the white rabbit. Said the littlest rabbit, "If I decided to vote one way on this matter, would you vote against me?" to the white rabbit. Whereupon the white rabbit said, "no I would not choose to vote against you, but I would choose to retain my right, as a rabbit, to vote in favour of the direction I thought best!"

"In that case", said the littlest rabbit, "I am going to vote in favour of that direction", which happened to be a left turn. In light of this decisive vote, white rabbit said, "if that direction is good enough for you, then it is also good enough for me". So off plodded our bunch of rabbits. The hastier rabbits were driving on at the front while the white rabbit and the littlest rabbit held back and started to chat. The white rabbit was quite impressed that the littlest rabbit had a lot of quite interesting things to say, and the littlest rabbit was quite interested in the stories white

rabbit had to tell, and quite impressed about how he
learned about his steering ears, when he was a little

white rabbit in the days when little white rabbit muffin was very tasty.

A good time later, the rabbits came to a part of the river which opened out into a pond type affair, on which the other side was held up by a wall of sticks and ground. In the middle of the pond was a big white swimming bird with a big white long smooth neck to its head. When the swimming bird saw the rabbits, it flipped a sort of how do you do, and in doing so, briefly showed off some fantastic white wings. The rabbits could see, even from a distance, that one of the white wings alone was bigger than six of the rabbits standing head to tail on all feet. "My name iss SSSwan, what do they call you?" said the bird to the rabbits.

The littlest rabbit piped up, "Oh we are rabbit's, and we're out for a little walk today", anxious to make an impression on the swan. The white rabbit went on to say, "Yes we are all out for a walk, and now we are all looking for a way to get to the other side of the river."

The swan raised one of his eyebrows on hearing that comment and said, "well if the other sside of the river iss where you need to be, you could perhapss walk on the wall the beaversss left over there. Mind you, from what I can ssee at thiss angle, iss that both ssidess look pretty much the ssame . . . of the river that iss".

"But our feet are terribly small, and as rabbits we would probably not stay as rabbits if we fell in the river!" said the littlest rabbit.

"Did the beavers ever come back after they built that wall thingy?" asked the white rabbit, of the swan.

"They do indeed, now and again, just to check that the river iss sstill held up by their wall, which ssometimess it issn't. If there happened to be a bit missssing, ussuallly because thiss sside of the river iss bigger than that sside, the beaverss would happily go about putting another bit where the misssing bit ussed to be", said the swan.

"Oh I see" said the white rabbit whose mind was rapidly closing in on an evolutionary theory involving walls, rivers, digging, burrowing and moving drink running through the meadow which as yet did not happen. Whereupon the littlest rabbit shyly asked the swan if it would be at all possible for a lift on her back to the other side of the river. The other rabbits who by now were still amazed at the view they had seen, which they had never seen before thus keeping them silent in awe, suddenly perked up their ears on hearing the littlest rabbit's suggestion, which in turn made the swan perk up her ears.

"I ssupposse I could" droned the swan. The littlest rabbit went on to say "No I should explain first, you see, a little while back down the river we took a vote about which direction to take, where it was decided that we as rabbits should continue along the river in an effort to look for a way to get to the other side, and looking at that wall, it seems that it would be far safer to hop on your back to achieve our aim".

"I ssee" said the swan, "and what might a vote be?"

"A vote is where we as rabbits ask a question, and then we each answer our question. Then we count up the answers, and the biggest answer wins because that way no one answer is more correct than another and no one rabbit gets the blame for doing something stupid", said the littlest rabbit.

"Oh in that casse would you like to hop on my back?" asked the swan

"In short I would very much like to see what it's like to move around the river in your eyes, but in long we are out walking as a group and your vote to carry me across the river doesn't necessarily mean that we as rabbits need to be on that side of the river", said littlest rabbit.

The swan smiled "for your clevernesss, I think you deserve that. It might sshut you up for a little bit and give the other rabbitss a chance to ssay something asswell".

"Thank you" said the littlest rabbit hopping on the great white swimming bird's back. When the four silent rabbits saw the littlest rabbit laughing very loudly on the graceful swans back they did say,

- I want a go next

- no it's my turn next, I'm older

- no me!

And

- I'm scared.

White rabbit was contented that at least his littlest rabbit could hold a conversation . . . at least.

After all the rabbits who wanted a go, had a go, the swan walked up on the river bank and sat amongst the rabbits and said, "now that you've sseen a ssafe way to get to the other sside of the river, would you care for a vote on that matter, sseeing ass you have come thiss far?"

The rabbit who said he was scared said he would like to go home, so the swan said "O.K. A going home vote insstead!" The littlest rabbit then piped up, "I think

we should have a stay here and talking to sswan vote!" The white rabbit said he agreed with the littlest voter. "Eh do I vote sso?" asked the swan who couldn't but stay with herself and wasn't quite sure if she could talk to herself. Another vote for a going home vote popped up from somewhere else, added to by a I'm hungry vote. The white rabbit noticed that the littlest rabbit's ears were not pointing in the same direction and said "I think that given all the different votes, that I'll take all those rabbits home who want to go home, and all those who want to stay can stay." It wasn't long till the swan heard a few goodbyes and was left to a conversation with the littlest rabbit, who had a bit of a squeaky voice.

"Do you often get out of the river?" asked the littlest rabbit

"Well you ssee, ass a sswan, I can sswim, dive, walk and fly and each are different wayss of moving to a different place. But when I'm in the ssky or in the river it iss very hard to not move, whereass when I'm not walking on the ground, I'm stuck in the one place, and all the things I would normally see moving, move in a different way".

"What is it like to fly?" asked the littlest rabbit, before interrupting himself to ask, "is it the same as swimming?"

The swan thought for a bit then replied, "Do you know I don't think I could put it into words but they are not the same as each other, because it is hard to move slowly in the sky, and it is hard to move quickly in the water. Diving is slower still".

"Well I must say, when you took me around that pond, the view did move smoothly and gracefully", complimented the littlest rabbit.

"Why thank you", said the swan, "it might look ssmooth and graceful on top of the water, but underneath it is a much different sstory. My feet have to thrassh and ssplassh to keep me moving my own way rather than the river'ss way, whereass if I'm flying, my wingss flap quite ssmootly and the windss thrassh and sswassh underneath me. But when I walk, I waddle".

"How smoothly do you take to the air so?" asked the littlest rabbit as he had never before this day seen a swan much less one fly.

"Thatss a very cumberssome tassk altogether. When I'm in the water, it is much harder to do than when on land but once I'm moving fast enough, all I have to do is lift up my feet, and I'm flying. Sso when I'm taking off from the water I have to battle with the river and the air, but when Im taking off from land, I only have to battle the air, if there iss nothing in the way of coursse", said the swan.

"Do you think you would be able to take off, fly and land with me on your back safely?", challenged the littlest rabbit.

"Well I have never tried ssuch a thing before, probably becausse I have never met an animal before who wass either sso brave or sso sstupid!" said the swan.

"Shall we have a vote?", beemed the littlest rabbit.

"O.K. Ssilly little thing, I vote no"

"Well I vote yes and that's a bigger word, so therefore it is a bigger answer and neither of us can take the blame for following the bigger answer", debated the littlest rabbit.

"O.K. You win", droned the swan, "hop on!". With that the littlest rabbit bounced on to the back of the swan and lodged his front paws onto the underside of the swan's neck feathers. The swan tried to dissuade the littlest rabbit one more time before the two went thundering down the river bank. The littlest rabbit bounced violently but still managed to hold on tightly, and with a daring leap, the swan jumped into the air.

"YAHHHOOOOOOOOOOOO!" screamed the littlest rabbit with blood racing through his whole everybit. They climbed higher into the sky to where the littlest rabbit could see high above the trees to all the life of all the forest and the meadow.

"Where will we go now?", asked the white swan. "Well would you like to come to my house for tea?", invited the littlest rabbit. The vote was carried. The two hovered around the meadow a bit until they saw where the rabbit house was. The swan came to nearby and landed, whereupon the littlest rabbit lost his grip and rolled on to the ground with a big bounce. "Ouch!", he bellowed as he sat up and rubbed the sore bump on his rump.

"White rabbit came out from the hole to see what all the fuss was, and when he saw the littlest rabbit and the swan there giggling, he said, "I'm not going to bother asking what is going on, would you two care for some dinner?"

Chapter 7

Pixie Pod was out doing Pixie type things one day, possibly a Grimpday, when he met his good friend Tree Topper Clive. "Oh there you are Pod!", said the very jovial squirrel who didn't seem so jovial today, "I need to have a word with you".

"Hello yourself", said Pixie Pod, "what is it that needs a word?"

- Well word has it, on the nutvine that is, that at least one of the river rats has eaten a meadow mouse and if this trend grows, I have been thinking, the river rats might get bigger, and the meadow mice will be all eaten up. So then there won't be any more meadow mice to eat, and the river rats might try other dinners such as the odd squirrel or somesuch.

- That's a big problem indeed, said Pixie Pod, mind you I'm sure the meadow mice are more worried that they are all going to get eaten up, than they would be worried about what the river rats are going to munch on after the completed wipe out of meadow mice.

- True, said Tree Topper Clive

-    Shall we go and give out to the river rats, or shall we go and console the meadow mice, asked Pixie Pod of Tree Topper Clive.

-    I was thinking that myself only I got quite scared of the notion that the river rats might confuse me for a meadow mouse with a bigger tail, and put me in their pie for Grimpday, said the squirrel before continuing, what if I went and consoled the meadow mice and you went to the river rats.

-    Sounds good to me, said Pixie Pod

So the two set off in opposite directions, Pod off to the forest, where the river was, and Clive off in search of wherever the field mice might be that day, probably hiding.

Pixie Pod knew the whole of the forest and the meadow very well so it didn't take him long to find the river rats scurrying around the river and its banks.

-    Who ate the meadow mouse? Shouted Pod quite matter of factly

The river rats who had been minding their own businesses at the time all looked up at the amusing Pixie, and a few of the rats grinning in a bunch shouted over,

-    We did, and what of the tasty little it

-        Well what would you normally eat? Asked Pod

-        Eh normally we wouldn't eat meadow mice, it's just that day we didn't fancy bird eggs, or frog spawns, or even tasty Pixies, said the ugliest rat.

-        Well I'll have you know mr or mrs ugly rat, whichever you are, that you never have nor never will eat a Pixie, and so you will never know how tasty they are, said Pixie Pod.

-        How do you know growled the lying rat

-        Because I am the only Pixie in all of the forest and the meadow, and no one has ever eaten me, and with a pixie blink he was standing on the other side of the river, just to show that the river rats need not trouble their minds about eating pixies, as they were not fast enough.

-        So what about not eating meadow mice either, asked Pixie Pod of the culprits.

-        Can you give us any good reason why we should do as you ask, asked the ugly rat, but not in a growling way.

-        I can, said Pixie Pod, you see if you eat all the meadow mice up, then there won't be any meadow mice left, and you'll probably be so used to eating mice animals by then, that you'd probably start eating other types of animals and get even bigger. Then when you rats have eaten all the animals in the whole of the forest and the meadow, you won't have anything to eat but yourselves, and then where would you be?

-        That's a very good reason actually Mr Pixie, said the ugliest rat. I suppose we should go back to eating bird eggs and frog spawns all the time.

-        Well, if it wouldn't upset you too much, added the pixie, and it wouldn't hurt to send some sort of apology to the meadow mice to help them trust you river rats not to do anything like that again.

-        O.K, said the ugly river rat, what if you and me go and find the meadow mice, and I'll say sorry.

-        Fine by me, said Pixie Pod, and the two set off.

As they walked through the meadow, Clive's bouncing tail was nowhere to be seen, so Pod thought he was probably lost looking for meadow mice in the forest. He must have been right, because soon they found the mice, in the meadow, of course, and they hadn't seen head not tail of Tree Topper Clive all day. The river rat gave a pathetic apology coupled with a promise to forbid it amongst river rats to eat anything other than what they normally would eat.

The main mouse, for his gallant part, forgave the river rats' impulsive eating and mentioned that the ill fated mouse did happen to be "the black gerbil" of the family. So all things considered, the peace treaty between the river rats and the meadow mice was a downright farce. Pixie Pod however was the only Pixie in the whole of the forest and the meadow, and as witness to such a chat between animals was the driving force for Peace, or more correctly for the stopping of meadow mice ending up on dinner plates.

When it was all over, Pixie Pod went back to his mushroom house, where he found Tree Topper Clive, sitting waiting for him . . .

"Ah Pod, there you are. I need a word?"

-        Does it involve river rats, meadow mice and dinners, inquired the weary and hungry Pixie

-        Well, no actually, it involves beavers, fishes and river walls really and . . .

Pixie Pod cut Tree Topper Clive short, saying

-        Good, in that case, i'm going inside to fill my tummy with tea and muffin, and if you are willing to forget all the problems in all the forest and the meadow, you can come in for some as well, otherwise go and solve all the problems for all of the whole of the forest and the meadow yourself".

Clive joined Pod for tea and muffin.

Chapter 8

Hernibia hedgehog had caught a very bad dose of the nellies, and in the days of all the forest and the meadow, when an animal had the nellies, there was only one cure. The trouble was, Hernibia didn't know she had the nellies, much less knew what the cure was. Normally you could tell an animal had the nellies if the animal had a runny nose and a sore tummy in windy weather. When Pixie Pod had the nellies once, he nearly blew up. Anyhow Hernibia had developed hedgehog type nellies and her best friend, Nianarbit could only think to say nasty things like "mind you don't sneeze on my sneezables". Nianarbit was quite a spikeful sort of a hedgehog, in that she would only say nice things to the animals she thought were importants. She would only say nasty things if she had to. Hernibia still had the nellies, and Nianarbit was the only one she knew to ask for help, or an insult.

-        "ACHOO . . . ACHOO . . . ACHOO . . . . I bwish I bwiddent feel like the bway I boo feel" sighed Hernibia.

-        "Well I don't feel the same way as you, so whatever you do, I still feel as good as new", said Nianarbit.

-        "Bwhich one bwas bnew, the bwon that you felt, or the bwone that you doo", asked Hernibia.

-        "I bnown't know, I just know that because I feel new, I dont go Achoo, like you do", answered Nianarbit.

-        "I don't blike the Achoos in much the blame bway blat you don't like the Achoos", said Hernibia.

-        "Bwell it bwasn't me blat gave them to you", said Nianarbit, before thinking and saying, "Did I say that?"

-        "You blid!", said Hernibia.

-        "What blid I blay?" asked Nianarbit, anxious to know what Hernibia heard because she knew what she meant.

-        "You said, bwell it bwasn't me blat gave them to you, I believe", replied Hernibia.

-        "No I blidn't, I bled, well it wasn't me that gave them to you, so I blid!", snapped Nianarbit.

-        "I know thats what you said", said Hernibia.

-       "I blidn't blay blat at all", growled Nianarbit.

-       "You did, you said it wasn't your fault that I had the Achoos, which I already knew because I had the Achoos before I met you", said Hernibia.

-       "I bliddent say anybling, I blid an Achoo, which I blobably blot from blu", said Nianarbit.

-       "But I didn't give you anything", said Hernibia, "I didn't even touch you, and anyway, I'm hungry", before curling up into a spikey ball and rolling the path in search of dinner.

-       "Nianarbit was strangely feeling more cross and intolerant than ever, and everytime she thought of something cross to say, an Achoo came out, even though there was no one to Achoo to. Nianarbit achooed her way right across the meadow until her nose got runny and she got sore in her tummy, so she had to sit down.

After a while of achooing and sitting, Pixie Pod happened to boulder by.

-        "Hello Nianarbit", chirped Pod.

-        "Hello Blixy Blod", grumbled Nianarbit.

-        "I beg your pardon?", said Pixie Pod, taking a step or two back from the hedgehog.

-        "I bled hello", restated Nianarbit with a large sticky bit growing from her cold pointy hedgehog nose.

-        "Yes I thought you said hello, in fact, I'm sure that I heard you say it, so I had to check just in case, you understand, said Pod with another step back.

-        "No, I'm bnot sure I unbersband Mr Bixie", said Nianarbit almost crying.

-        "Why you have a dose of the nellies, you poor little spikey thing", sympathised Pixie Pod.

-        "The neblies?"

-        "No the nellies", furthered Pod.

-        "And how bo I get rib off theb", asked Nianarbit, hoping there was an instant cure.

-        "Oh you don't get rid of them, you give them away", said Pixie Pod as he remembered himself the awful he had when he himself was nellie bound.

-        "But who in all of be borest band be beadow bwould bwant these neblies", asked Nianarbit, who couldn't really understand why any animal, even the very stupidest ones, would ever have a need for the nellies.

- "That's a bery good question", said Pod who instantly realised what he had said and took another step backwards.

- "Any bore of those backward steps and you bwill have to bout", grumbled Nianarbit.

- "Yes I know, but at this time of my life, I could really do without your nellies, whatever steps necessary", explained Pixie Pod before going on to say, "if you manage to find something that likes nellies, you can give it to them, and they might even give you something that you'd like".

- "Achoo !", went Nianarbit which instantly made Pixie Pod disappear.

- "Oh no, I've achooed Pixie Pod away and I don't know where I'd find anything that would like my nellies", cried Nianarbit. With that a Snoopytrible called out, "I say, you wouldn't want to know anyone with unwanted nellies, would you?"

- "Bo you bwant mine?" hoped the hedgehog.

- "Oh, Yes Bleeese, thanks", said the Snoopytrible.

- "What would be terribly blice for you to bnow in return?"

-        "Bwell I bwouldn't blind knowing how to be friends with Hernibia again?", said Nianarbit.

-        "Bwell why don't you go and say hello to her so", said the snoopytrible.

-        "Will my nellies be gone then?" Perked up the hedgehog.

-        "Well I should imagine if they aren't there now they brobably wouldn't be there then", confirmed the Snoopytrible.

Chapter 9

It was a bit of a dull day in the forest and the meadow and Pixie Pod was having a daydreaming meander along what is commonly referred to as Madaboo lane. As he turned another acorn filled corner on this lane when he suddenly came across a Splitzploo making a funny noise. Now the Splitzploo wasn't actually making the noise himself or herself, (you can never be too sure with Splitzploos), moreover the animal was blowing into a bag and putting its fingers on different parts of a holey stick coming out the other side. Each time the Splitzploo's fingers moved, a different noise would come out of the instrument.

- "What do you be doing?", inquired the pixie of the Splitzploo.

- "I'm practising!", growled the Splitzploo, angry that he had been interrupted.

- "Oh, I see! And what are you practising for?", asked Pixie Pod thinking that the Splitzploo obviously needed a lot of practice if he were intent on turning that racket into music.

- "For the free festival of Madaboo and pan", grunted the Splitzploo.

-     "If it's a free festival, does that mean my friend the squirrel Tree Topper Clive and myself Pixie Pod could attend?", asked Pixie Pod, anxious to be part of anything that could mean fun.

-     "No, it's only for Splitzploos", the Splitzploo said in very cross tones altogether.

-     "And when is this festival?" the pixie asked.

-     Tomorrow night!" said the Splitzploo still cross for no reason at all.

With that Pixie Pod left the Splitzploo alone and headed for Tree Topper Cllive's tree top home, with the purpose of discussing trying to attend a festival to which they were clearly not invited and more to the point would clearly not be welcome. When Pod reached the Grimpalong he threw a few acorns up at the doorway to try and attract Tree Topper Clive's attentions.

After a while Tree Topper Clive appeared at the door and chirped, "Oh hello Pod!"

-     "Hello there Clive, I've just discovered something and I've had an idea about it I think you'd like", said the pixie quite enthusiastically.

-     "Really and what does this idea involve?", asked Tree Topper Clive, ever hesitant about Pixie Pod's ideas.

-        Well it's like this . . . I met a Splitzploo down Madaboo lane and he was practising on a funny noise machine for the free festival of Madaboo and Pan, which, he was quite insistent, was only for Splitzploos. So I was thinking we could go along to this festival and hide in the trees. That way we could enjoy the festival without upsetting the Splitzploos, said Pixie Pod, turning red in the face as he was quite out of breath explaining the whole thing to Tree Topper Clive. When he got his breath back, he went on to say, "It's on tomorrow night, what do you think about going?"

-        "Won't the Splitzploos be angry if they catch us? said the squirrel, always anxious about peril of any sort, including the wrath of Splitzploos.

-        "They won't, we will be clever about it", said Pixie Pod.

-        "Right, you're on", said Tree Topper Clive.

        The following evening, the two friends met at Pixie Pod's mushroom house and prepared for the night's festivities by putting some Gloobleberry muffin in a handkerchief and making a flask of puddle water tea. Squirrels and especially Pixies are quite partial to puddle water tea. When all was ready, the two set off in the direction of Madaboo lane.

When they got close to the lane, they could hear the Splitzploos tuning their instruments. "I think it's time we got up into the trees", suggested Pixie Pod. "I'm a good tree for viewing festivals", came a voice from the dense wood. Tree Topper Clive hiccupped at this time, so he didn't hear the talking tree. Anyhows the pair scuttled up a tree and got a perfect view of a gamut of Splitzploos.

The tuning of the Splitzploo's instruments was beginning to give Pod the idea that he shouldn't have bothered but then a loud bell rang out and there was a silence for as far as the ear could hear, and a stout Splitzploo began to proclaim an ancient tribal rhyme which basically referred to the fact that it was time for the free festival of Madaboo and Pan to start . . . and then it did.

Forty tremendous Splitzploo windbags began bellowing out a thunderous noise and the forest began to shake.

"Holy Moly!!!", though Tree Topper Clive as the branch he was sitting on began to wobble and if Pixie Pod wasn't there with him, he'd probably be quite afraid.

"As the noise continued, a strange melody began to develop that lulled the soul and the mind and one by one the Splitzploos fell under the spell and started to fall asleep. The more Splitzploos that fell asleep, the less windbags were being blown until there was one Splitzploo left blowing away to his heart's content.

Pixie Pod wondered aloud, that even though there was only one Splitzploo left the noise was still scary and it was lucky only Splitzploos were invited, and only Splitzploos would really appreciate the racket. Certainly it seemed it was only the Splitzploos that were affected by the spells of the noise which included the last remaining Splitzploo which then keeled over with a magical stupor.

Chapter 10

It was late in the nut season and nuts were scarce on the ground by this stage. Clive had been collecting nuts on and off due to the fact he was usually busy with Pixie Pod. This meant by the time the cold season would have gotten ridiculously cold, Clive's hibernation would have turned to hungernation. Pod had mentioned to Tree Topper Clive that there would be an endless supply of Gloobleberry muffin should his nuts dry up but the squirrel was sceptical about the nature of the magic spells the Pixie was mixing in his muffins this weather, so he decided to resume his nut hunt.

Tree Topper Clive headed for the nuttiest part of the forest singing a song in his head which was basically the recipe for nut a la king to the tune of pixieland skies. Seeing as nut a la king was quite an intricate concoction the song was longer than 16 verses with no chorus to be heard. Clive had just reached the part of the song where you had to milk something with udders for the sauce when a harmony to his lyric began and made the music sound really quite beautiful, whatever about the theme.

When the song ended the most elegant squirrel Clive had ever seen scarpered down from a nearby oak and introduced herself to Tree Topper Clive as Irgaan and in turn Clive introduced himself as himself. Both animals had somehow strangely managed to overcome their respective habitual shyness and talk at length on squirrel type subjects, being two attractive young squirrels.

After a while it transpired that the two had spent some of their formative years playing in the same part of the forest but as everyone knows, squirrels don't start talking until they are quite mature, so that is why their names were not familiar to each other.

Tree Topper Clive said, "You have a beautiful name Irgaan, what does it mean?"

She replied softly, "It means creature of tenderness"

Irgaan didn't continue with the same question to Clive as she was an expert in not labouring the obvious, but instead asked how his nut store was at this stage of the nut season.

"Oh desperate! Desperate! I'll be half the squirrel I am now by the end of the cold season if I don't get on with stocking up"

"There is a lot of squirrels in your predicament", said Irgaan. I think it might be that because some pixie or other managed to convince the river rats not to eradicate the mice population, so they have taken to eating nuts instead", enlightened Irgaan.

"That's Pod!" blurted Tree Topper Clive.

"No it's quite true", said Irgaan.

"Hmmm", thought Clive.

Irgaan didn't bother to continue to attempt to convince Clive that it was true as she hated arguments and strong words but it did occur to her that Pod was a funny way of dismissing a theory.

"Come", she said, "I know a tree the river rats haven't yet ransacked. I'll take you there". And she led him down Fern path.

For a while the two scuppered and scarpered with squirrel agility to a point in the forest quite a way away from the river, then suddenly Irgaan called on Clive to stop, which he did with a skid.

"Can you smell the harvest on the breeze?" she asked.

Clive could sense there was food in the area but as he was looking up into the trees, it took him a short time for his eyes to become uncrossed and actually grasp the fact he would not starve this winter.

"Are you relying on these?", asked Tree Topper Clive of Irgaan.

"No Clive, I have what I need, take what you want or even what you need but not what you don't need, in case there are any other tummy hungry squirrels in the forest.

"If you took a bundle and I too, then I wouldn't have any less than I need and we wouldn't have to come back", suggested an elated Tree Topper Clive.

"Ok Clive, I'll help you", said Irgaan, looking at him, and for the first time Clive caught the gaze of her kind eyes.

By the time Irgaan and Clive reached the Grimpalong, Clive had a courageous question for Irgaan. Clive put the food down in the corner of the Grimpalong and then stood and looked at Irgaan, then looked at the walls, then the ceiling, then the walls again, then at Irgaan again, and back to the walls . . .

Irgaan broke the impass by saying, "you have a nice home".

Clive's courage index reached its maximum setting and blurted out loudly and quickly, "would you like to be friends?"

Irgaan said, "Sure, I thought we were already".

The chivalrous squirrel then said, "Yes but Irgaan, would you like to be best friends?"

Irgaan said, "Yes Clive, I'd love to be best friends".

Chapter 11

Pixie Pod was trying to cast a magic spell for five nights and he wasn't having much luck. He came up with the spell notion a long time ago but it was at this time he felt if the spell was cast, there would be untold wonder and uplifting bemusement for all.

He first tried the spell in his food, then when that didn't seem to work, he tried it in the air, by blowing, floating, wisping and so on. Then he tried whispering funny words that seemed to come from a strange part of his head, which knowing Pixies, was not unexpected. "DAEPA DAEPA"

But that particular spell he discovered made the green spiky nuts grow on the trees in the wrong season, which if cast regularly, would put unease in the hearts of quite a few of the animals who prepared to go for a long sleep when that sort of thing starts happening. Still it's handy when you accidently discover accidental spells like that.

On one of the nights a tune came into his head that was soul piercingly beautiful and each note sent imaginary sparks out in all directions, but it still wasn't the spell he wanted. It was a lovely tune though.

After eating a muffin so light, it was nearly invisible one morning, he went out and sat by the river and toyed with the ripples and was casually turning them into splashes when he saw a stone at the edge of the water.

"I know that stone", thought Pod. "I know that Pixie" thought the stone. Suddenly a splash turning into a ripple distracted Pixie Pod and when he looked back, the stone had disappeared. It's not widely known that stones generally don't hang around for long magic spell consultations with pixies. They feel that really the more apt approach is to try and teach yourself so they don't get the blame for situations like the trees turning pink or the grass puce.

At one stage, Pod put two flowers in the ground side by side and threw an old familiar spell on them to make them grow, rather than having to return every so often to see if they had grown enough for him. So as they were dancing in the breeze he made them glow and whispered 'dair rud ao gra'. But this didn't work because the flowers just grew back into the ground.

Pixies believe that because time doesn't stand still, there's no point in sitting back and watching it. So Pod thought he'd have a go at making it sit still to see if it would be a more comfortable atmosphere to watch it. No use. No sooner had he coaxed time into reclining in a relaxing pose when time itself got bored and life got heavy. The river's gurgle became a gugle and the whistle of the leaves became a hush. So Pod gave time a tickle, and time stood up and made off again.

On the fifth day he gave up. It saddened him that since Pixies brought magic to the world when time began, that the magic hadn't changed, and because Pixies don't get angry, all the magic was white magic. So with no new magic spells to cast, Pixie Pod cast an old spell to make something new. Dabsins Visti Owbat Svia; Then the leaves under a nearby tree rolled around into a ring and sparks of crazy light spat from the middle as the funniest animal you could think of, grew out of where the light sparks spat.

Fully formed, Pixie Pod called it a Gibblebund.

Chapter 12

Tree Topper Clive was dandering along a pliver pluddle plondly plow one stormy morning and its neither here nor there nor anywhere but the plondly plow was more pliver pluddle than anything else. Eventually he came to a point in this pliver pluddle where there was another pliver pluddle plondly plow of a smaller size growing into the bigger one, right in front of him.

Thus the only way forward was to walk on. He took one step into the flowing watery plondly plow and his foot became very cold. He knew he didn't like the feeling, but in any event he knew he must continue stepping onwards if he was to finish his journey. So he took another step so that both ankles were at this stage under water. He could feel the strong current of the water but it didn't stop him thinking he should go on. He took two more steps, once with the left foot then with the right, so he was up to his knees in it at this stage. The current felt stronger but probably wasn't. After yet another pair of steps his waist was wet, the current felt stronger and he wasn't halfway there. Then the unluckiest thing that could happen a squirrel happened. He took one more step and was gobbled by the pliver pluddle plondly plow.

It was upsetting at first because he was submerged, but with the frantic instinctive swirling of his little squirrel hands he managed to get his head above the water, where he could breathe again. Once he achieved this, he began saying "Holy Moly" an awful lot, and very quickly, mind you.

It must have been something to do with the number of "Holy Molys" he was saying because after a while a large branch was floating by. Tree Topper Clive reached out with all his might and caught onto the branch, and once he did so he overcame one of his problems, the paddling one. Still his breathing was terribly heavy. He nearly drowned after all. And so for a while he floated down the by now very big pluddle plondly plow catching his breath back.

When he finally caught his breath back, he found he had another problem, and that was, it was frightfully cold in the plondly plow. He began to shiver and his teeth began to rattle. The only thing he could think to do was to try and climb on top of the large branch and see if it could hold a small squirrel on top of the water.

With a tremendous squirrel heave, he heaved one of his tiny legs around the trunk end of the branch, and with one deft squirrel-like motion, he was hugging the branch from the top side. "Whoa!", he thought to himself, as he thought about where he was and what he was doing. He sat up and gave his furry skin a good shake, so that all the water in his fur flew off him, in all directions. He didn't feel so cold then. The branch bobbed down the pliver pluddle plondly plow, with a Tree Topper Clive happily admiring the view as they passed familiar parts of all of the forest and the meadow.

The next thing the sometimes dense squirrel thought to do was to try and stand up on the branch. So leaning forward carefully he grabbed the bow of the branch with his two front mits and gently put himself in the upright position. Then even more carefully he let go with his two front mits and stood up. "Whoa! Wayhay! Yihee! There was all sorts of happyness and funny noises coming from the middle of the plondly plow. This probably could have been one of the happier times in the little squirrel's life. And that counts for something when you consider the number of adventures he was fortunate enough to have experienced.

The standing up on the branch lasted for some time and Tree Topper Clive was beginning to get a tiny bit bored with the whole thing. He wanted to sit down again, just to make sure he didn't fall off, So he leaned down and grabbed the branch with his front paws. But as he did so, the branch dipped to one side in the water which made it swerve in the general direction of one of the banks. "Holy Moly", thought Tree Topper Clive, I can get back onto dry land if I can continue to make the branch go in this direction. So he continued to lean on the branch and the branch continued in the general direction of the bank.

After about five minutes of this, the branch
beached itself on the side of the pliver pluddle plondly
plow. Tree Topper Clive stepped off the branch into the
water and he found he was waist deep in it again. With a
number of steps very much quicker than when he was
getting himself into this mess, he headed out of the water
and back onto dry land squirrels know and cherish.

Chapter 13

Tree Topper Clive woke up one morning and it
was the sort of morning that he would have fallen on the
floor, only Grimpalongs don't have floors and Clive slept
at the bottom of his. He got up and went out onto his
branch just outside his Grimpalong to eat some nuts for
breakfast and watch the sun come up over the trees.
Suddenly even though the sun hadn't come up yet, Tree
Topper Clive saw Pixie Pod walking towards him but he
couldn't believe it, as it was much too early for the lazy
Pixie Pod that Clive knew to be walking around the
forest. I mustn't have woken up yet, Clive thought to
himself. "You have", whispered the tree, which surprised
Tree Topper Clive so much he fell out of his perch and
bounced bum first on the ground.

"Clive, something terrible has happened", said a very troubled Pixie Pod.

"You're telling me?" replied the incredibly confused squirrel, who wasn't sure if he was talking to Pixie Pod, the tree or even if it had all been a dream and he was still asleep in the Grimpalong.

"You mean you know already?", asked Pod.

"No I'm not sure I do!" replied Clive.

"Well when I was asleep I dreamt that a river grew in the meadow, so I woke up and went to the meadow, and sure enough, there was a river there", said Pixie Pod.

"But why would a river grow there", asked the totally confused Clive who began wondering if the sun was going to come up at all today? And if it should really bother at all? Then Clive remembered the idea white rabbit mentioned to him and went "UH OH! Pod I think we should have breakfast first before we get on with today".

"Maybe you are right", said Pixie Pod as the two went up into the Grimpalong for breakfast, which happened to be nuts.

By the time breakfast was over, the sun had come up and Tree Topper Clive asked Pixie Pod to show him where the river had got too in the meadow. Pixie Pod was still quite worried at this stage because he could feel the nuts in his tummy, so he knew it wasn't a dream.

The river had always just been in the forest and now it didn't. Clive thought the river had always been in

the forest for a reason but if it wasn't just only in the forest anymore, things would be different. Pod thought that now the river was in the forest and the meadow at the same time, it might mean that there were going to be more animals in the meadow than there were in the forest. Then underneath the sunrise the two friends saw the river going through the meadow, and it looked like all the animals from all of the forest and the meadow were sitting or standing or flying or swimming or wading, in or around the river.

- "Holy Moly!" said Tree Topper Clive

- "I bleg your blardon?" said Pixie Pod, who didn't realise he sounded like he had a few nellies.

It really looked quite spectacular, you see. As the two got nearer the river, it looked like everything including the corn, the birds and the clouds had some sort of a way of looking at the new path."

- "I think this looks fabulastic!", thought Tree Topper Clive.

'M M M M M M M M M M M M M M M M M M M" thought Pixie Pod.

But why is nobody talking or singing or anything, thought Tree Topper Clive, who probably would normally hear something other than a river in this part of the meadow at this time of the morning.

"M M M M M M M M M M M M M M M M M M M", thought Pixie Pod.

- "What do you think?" asked Tree Topper Clive.

"M M M M M M M" Pixie Pod didn't say.

Clive could see Pod was too overcome and he couldn't be too sure which overcame Pod, being up so early in the morning for once or seeing what the both could see.

-        "M M M M M M M M M M M M M M M M M M M M M M M M M M M M M M M M M", said Pixie Pod.

-        "M M M M M M M M M M M?" said Tree Topper Clive with a very peculiar look altogether.

"M M M", thought Pixie Pod.

"Ah M M M M M M", rethought Tree Topper Clive.

"M ",

"M ".

Pod and Clive sat down beside the river, but still didn't say anything. At that moment white rabbit did notice the two, with his steering ears, and went up beside them without taking his eyes off the river. After still a very long time, nobody had said anything, and it seemed as if it were a race not to be the first to say anything.

-	Where will we live now?

-	Were ever that you would like to

-	I can see the sun from here

-	We can get drinkings without going into the forest now

-	Will we have beaver walls in the meadow?

-	White rabbit will know if there are any more beaver walls due

-	I'm not really sure it was my idea to begin with

-	I'b blike to bknow more

-	Look at all the grass that didn't use to have river all over it

-	Look, the clouds are not getting in the way of the sun's view of the river's new path

-	Why doeammi ize ahurta whena lookatzee Sunna?

-	Clive, look at the mice children sitting with the rat children

	M M M

-        fair finty fole foff fe forest fand fe feadow fould foy find fall foff fe fanimals fofever fat fwon fime?

-        It sseems sstrange to sswim in the riverss path with no ssunbursstss

-        What's a Gloobleberry?

-        Iss that you off again littlest?

-        Look at those animals the sun is showing us under the river?

-        Oh o o o we o o o are o o o fiish o o o

-        Hello fiish

-        The meadow looks longer now

-        So does the forest

-        What shall we call this time?

M M M M M M M M M M M M M M M M M M M M M M M M M M M M M M M M M M M M M M M M M M M M M M M M M M M M M M M M M M M M M M M M M M M M M M M M M M M M M M M M M M M M M M M M

-        I must say, a moment like the present shouldn't be enjoyed without some Gloobleberry muffin for everyone, and some nuts

-        and some worms

-        and some fishes

-        and some river rats

-        and some foxes

-        and some nellies

-        I don't blink I could blive in the bliver.

Pod went off back to his mushroom house to make a big supply of muffin for his lunch and anyone else who cared for any. Tree Topper Clive began talking about what the river would mean, now that it was in the meadow as well. The river rat children and the mice children started playing and even one rat child was showing a mice child how to swim. Mind you the little mouse did have its tail tied a hoop to a long piece of grass on the river's edge. The littlest rabbit was sitting on the swan's back, on the river. And the sun got higher in the sky. Nobody was quite sure of what M M M M . . . . meant, but they think they all did at the time. One of the birds in the sky even looked like Napaleen.

Pixie Pod returned a little whiles later with a great bag of muffin for everybody, if they liked. The Snoopytrible said "thank you very much" as he picked up a muffin which looked like it had something special in the Gloobleberry department, but at the same time pretending not to notice.

The main meadow mouse inquired as to what the recipe might be for Gloobleberry muffin to which he was given the reply, "I'm not entirely sure, but I do realise when it does become Gloobleberry muffin".

"Aha I see, I say Tree Topper Clive, could you ever happen to tell me if Pixie Pod happened to tell you the recipe for Gloobleberry muffin?" "No I don't think I could, for he has never told it to me and I couldn't write it down if I did hear, because squirrels can't write."

"I can write", said Pixie Pod.

"Oh Goody!", said the mouse, "would you write down for me, your recipe?"

"I surely would write down you the recipe", as he wrote "M M M M M M M M M" into the ground with a stick.

"But I'm not sure I can read or understand what that says?" said the littlest mouse. "Well you see I'm not really sure of the recipe myself but I think I remember what I usually put into the Gloobleberry muffin, but as I say, I think you always know when it is a Gloobleberry muffin", replied Pod. "Sometimes I can't get all the bits together at what I think is the right time, but it always seems to turn out OK." he continued.

- "Nuts are a very easy recipe Mr Mouse", said Tree Topper Clive chirpily.

- "Are they?" asked the tree.

-       "Well Yes actually, they are just as nice cooked as uncooked", furthered the mouse-like squirrel to the point of adding, "I wonder would the sun like muffin?"

"M M M M M M M M M M"

-       "I didn't", thought someone

-       "Didn't what?", thought someone else

-       "I didn't say that", said the someone

-       "But what did you think?", asked Tree Topper Clive, "when you first saw the river floating through the meadow."

o o o H O L Y o o o M O L Y o o o

"Herto with Glubble terwot,

Signed through the eye of a dot,

Bertwax doo bertwoxle and Drubble,

Wax doo blerbil, blerblax and berbroxil"

Yummy

-       "Is it in my head or in my tummy, that my feeling is peculiarly funny", said Pixie Pod to himself as he looked at his reflection in the river, "or is it purely a case of overmuffin"

-       bello blittle birl! Said the Snoopytrible

-       heblo

-       Would you blike somebing in return for your nellies?

- 	I would blike to say thank you and hello

A cat type animal came up to Pixie Pod and said "Hello Pixie Plip, I didn't expect to meet you at a party in this place"

Pixie Pod had never seen such an animal in his whole life before, and so it took him a while to answer that his name wasn't Pixie Plip but indeed Pixie Pod. "Oh I see" said the animal, "I must have confused you for someone else altogether, but I must say I am easily confused most times"

"I know what you mean" said PixiePod, "sometimes I get very confused myself altogether. In fact today, with the river and everything, It might be the most confusing day forever of the forest and the meadow."

"Now that you've mentioned it, I think I'm even more confused Plip", said the animal.

"Eh it's Pod actually", said the Pixie.

"Oh I see", said the animal before going on to ask about Gloobleberry muffin, which he thought quite tasty. Pixie Pod brought the animal to over where he had written the recipe down.

By this time, white rabbit went over to the beavers to compliment their ability to build river walls, whereupon they began plans for some sort of pond for the meadow, like there was in the forest, and the clouds had also moved on. So it was harder to see the grass under the river now in littlest rabbits eyes, whose ears were both pointing in the same direction. Nothing seemed to be done that day, only talking, and nothing seemed to be eaten that day, only Gloobleberry muffin. There was an air all the way across the whole of the forest and the meadow of a general calm and mirth. Tree Topper Clive looked up at the sun . . . .

-        Oh the sunny is going down

-        Maybe this day is quicker than other days usually do be

-        Maybe it's longer but we just think it's shorter

-        Does that mean the night time will be shorter than the long time?

-        I don't know

-        Blayblee bwee bould blay blear all blight blo blat blee ball bee brends bore eber

-        I'm getting cold mummy

-        Nuts anyone?

M M M M M M M M M M M M

M M M M M M M M M M M M

Good night Sun

Hello stars

Is there any more of that muffin left?

What will we do if the river isn't here in the morning?

o o W E o o W O N T o o B E o o H E R E o o

-     If it went away, we probably could bring it back, It would just mean more work, that's all.

M M M M M M

There's no reason why it all can't be the same

Chapter 14

The next morning Pixie Pod got out of bed at a completely different time to what he normally got up, and he even beat the sun to it, which was enough to put a smile on his face and reach for some muffin. The mushroom house had been left in a bit of a state and it was time to put it straight, Pod thought. When he finished making his bed, the sun came up and shone bright into his kitchen, by which time the kettle had boiled.

By the time the cocks did a doodle, Pixie Pod had finished all the cleaning up, and was muffin and mits out the door. Tree Topper Clive had already beaten him in checking the river was there still. But now the ever nutty squirrel was anxious to know if white rabbit and the beavers had met yet to decide anything constructive on the meadow pond matter. "Ah Pod, you haven't seen white rabbit anywhere, have you?" said Clive. "I haven't seen him, no, but I think I might have dreamt about him during the night", replied Pod.

"I blay! Blid blou blee blany sblare neblies anyblare?" the Snoopytrible happened to shout over.

"Sorry we couldn't help you there", was the reply from the other side of the river.

"Nice morning all the same"

"Indeed."

"Do you have anything to do today?" inquired Tree Topper Clive of Pixie Pod.

"No not really, it's just I'd had this idea of going to where the river used to be and seeing what it looked like now, in that part of the forest", replied Pixie Pod. And off the two plodded, to the last place they heard the beavers lived. Pixie Pod knew where he'd met a beaver three days previous, so it seemed a logical place to begin the search for the place they thought of. On the way, Pixie Pod said he wasn't sure if he was dreaming when he imagined the littlest rabbit flying at a great height on SSSwan's back which only seemed to provoke a 'HOLY

MOLY' type profanity from Tree Topper Clive's wisdom organs. A little while later, Clive went back on what he'd said and continued with a graphic picture of a free falling bunny without a spare set of wings. Which in turn, turned back into a holy moly type profanity. Pixie Pod resolved that he wouldn't delve further into the matter, and the two stumbled upon the place where the river used to be but isn't anymore.

Clive and Pod hopped and bounced along the muddy stone path on which the sun shone in another way. There wasn't much conversation at this while, as the two were concentrating on not falling on the slippery stones and hurting themselves, as that seemed more important.

Tree Topper Clive happened to notice a weeping beaver from the corner of his hopping and bouncing eye, which encouraged him to stop and say, "You wouldn't be a lost sort of a beaver would you?" The beaver weeper looked up to him and replied, "well I'm lost, and then one night, the river disappeared, and I got even more lost, so to speak."

Pixie Pod stopped and said, "I think I might know where there may be other beavers, if that's what you are looking for, or would that make you unlost?"

"Just go up the stones that way and take a turn when you see the river", said Tree Topper Clive, pointing to that way up the stones.

"Why would the beavers be in the meadow?" asked the glum beaver wiping his tears away.

"Do you know white rabbit?", inquired Pixie Pod.

"White rabbit?" asked the beaver.

"I thought not", said Tree Topper Clive quite matter-of-factly as he fell on his bum on a stone. The beaver had a bit of a giggle at this as it seemed quite funny to him at the time. Pixie Pod laughed a little louder than the giggle, which incited a great big loud hilarious laugh in Tree Topper Clive, which prevented him thinking about a sore bum.

After the funniness seemed to pass away, the beaver sniggered, "which way did you say the beavers were?", which almost seemed as if he had to force the words out. Clive was about to say 'that way' again, before he just started laughing out very loudly indeed, more so than before. The funnier it seemed, the funnier it was until the time Pod noticed that the trees stopped a little ways down the slippy stone path.

"Do you think we should go on down the path?" asked Tree Topper Clive.

"I think we should decide which way is this way and which way is that way anyway?", giggled Pixie Pod.

"I think the anyways are better anyways!", chortled the beaver.

"I think that if you have too much to think about at one time, then you might stop thinking about it", laughed Tree Topper Clive.

"Does anything incorporate everything?" paused the beaver

"Does everything co-operate with anything", unpaused Pixie Pod just as quickly.

"Where in all of the forest and the meadow would you get a giggle such as this" mentioned somebody but nobody but Pod was too sure who.

"Did you happen to bring any muffin with you, by the way" asked Tree Topper Clive, who hadn't looked up into the trees for nuts.

"I think I might perhaps have a muffin or two up my sleeve somewhere, if I look", replied the podded one, "would you like some?"

"Well yes but I reckon the big toothed one there could do with a bit of muffin", said the nutted one.

"Oh yes please", said the beaver

M M M

M M

M

~ La Fin ~